WOULD YOU RATHER GAME BOOK FOR KIDS

500 Hilarious Questions, Silly Scenarios and Challenging Choices the Whole Family Will Love

JENNY MOORE

Table of Contents

Introduction

What do you do when you spend time with your friends? Or what about your family? Do you play games – or do you just hang out?

Well, here's an idea.

How about you ask them questions!

Wait, just hear me out for a second.

What many people don't know is that questions are super important – especially when you are talking to your friends and family.

Questions help you learn more about the person you are talking to. And even more important, they also help the person you are talking to learn more about *you*.

Learning more about your friends and family is what helps build *connections*.

In short, it makes you better friends.

Now, in this book you will find a list of 500 amazing questions that will really help you get to know your friends and family better.

Have you ever wanted to know if mom would rather be a mermaid with the head of a fish, or a fish with the head of a mermaid? And what about dad? Have you ever wanted to know if he would rather read minds, or see into the future?

Well, now you can learn these things and heaps more.

Would You Rather Game Book for Kids is meant to have you (and your family) stretching the limits of your imagination. This means you need to answer every question as truthfully as possible – and make sure you have a whole lot of fun in the process.

With the four different sections, "What Would You Do?", "What Do You Have to Lose?", "What Could You Do?", and "What If?, you will have a blast laughing and learning from your family and friends.

So, without further ado, what would you rather?

Chapter 1

What Would You Do? Would You Rather?

At some point in your life, you have probably been asked the question, *"What would you do?"*

This question puts you in a funny situation and sees how you would react.

For example, could you live in this particular place, or do this crazy thing?

With the questions in this chapter, you will not only be able to imagine these crazy moments, but live them out. You might find yourself off adventuring in a faraway land, or doing something you would have never even imagined.

So, let's dive into the questions and see what adventures await!

Questions

1

Would you rather have a boat you can sail anywhere in or have a car you can drive anywhere in?

2

Would you rather live in the sky or in the sea?

3

Would you rather travel the world or fly to outer space?

4

Would you rather walk a mile with no shoes on or sit in a wooden chair for 24 hours straight?

5

Would you rather be stuck in a hurricane or a snow storm?

6

Would you rather climb the highest mountain or swim the depths of the oceans?

7

Would you rather eat the world's hottest pepper or stand barefoot on a frozen lake?

8

Would you rather swim in a pool of chocolate milk or drink a cup of public pool water?

9

Would you rather live with a wild pack of dogs or live in a swamp full of crocodiles?

10

Would you rather have a snowball fight with a polar bear or go on a horseback adventure?

11

Would you rather cook for the rest of your life or eat fast food for the rest of your life?

12

Would you rather always smell like oranges or always smell like apples?

13

Would you rather paint the world's biggest painting or make the world's biggest pancake?

14

Would you rather get a haircut every day of your life or never have another haircut again?

15

Would you rather live in a house made of cheesecake or live in a house made of lasagna?

16

Would you rather play video games in the White House or go deep sea diving to look for coral?

17

Would you rather live on a boat or live on an airplane?

18

Would you rather run everywhere you have to go or sleep-in whenever you wanted?

19

Would you rather have a house made of gold or a house made of diamonds?

20

Would you rather compete in the Olympics as a runner or compete as a jumper?

21

Would you rather swim with sharks or hunt with wolves?

22

Would you rather be the captain of a ship or the pilot of an airplane?

23

Would you rather be a police officer or a firefighter?

24

Would you rather grow up to be a doctor or a lawyer?

25

Would you rather be a flower that blooms only at night or a tree that grows moss on its limbs?

26

Would you rather drive or walk from Los Angeles to New York City?

27

Would you rather farm potatoes or raise cattle for a living?

28

Would you rather work on a shrimp boat or in an apple orchard?

29

Would you rather walk across a pit of hot coals or have a snowball fight with only a t-shirt on?

30

Would you rather build everything you own or buy everything you own?

31

Would you rather go to a scary movie with your mother or your grandmother?

32

Would you rather play a game of mini golf with George Washington or Abraham Lincoln?

33

Would you rather have an arm wrestling match with your mother or your father?

34

Would you rather eat oranges for every meal on the weekends or eat chopped liver for lunch every day?

35

Would you rather wait it out during a snowstorm or a hurricane?

36

Would you rather take a plane through the Bermuda Triangle or drive a car through Roswell, New Mexico?

37

Would you rather only write with crayons or pencils for the rest of your life?

38

Would you rather sleep on a sofa for the rest of your life or purchase a new bed every two months?

39

Would you rather communicate only through hand puppets or sing automatically whenever you tried to talk?

40

Would you rather the sun always be out or the moon always be out?

41

Would you rather eat spinach or cabbage for breakfast every day?

42

Would you rather clamp a clothespin on your nose every second of every day or live in a garbage dump for one day out of the month?

43

Would you rather sound like Donald Duck or Goofy whenever you speak?

44

Would you rather have the sun set at 3 P.M every day or 10 P.M every night?

45

Would you rather ride a scooter everywhere you go or bounce on a pogo stick everywhere you go?

46

Would you rather travel to Australia or Alaska?

47

Would you rather chop down trees by yourself with only an axe or take a bath once a month?

48

Would you rather live in an ant pile or live in a bird's nest?

49

Would you rather scream at the top of your lungs or whisper as softly as you could every time you talked?

50

Would you rather perform in a play wearing only your underwear or go without sunscreen for an entire trip to the beach?

51

Would you rather go bowling on an airplane or play frisbee on the moon?

52

Would you rather plant trees everywhere you go or eat dirt every day for a snack?

53

Would you rather eat cheese and onion sandwiches as your only meal for a month or would you rather dye your hair bright purple until it grows out?

54

Would you rather drink pickle juice instead of water or have everything you eat taste like pickles?

55

Would you rather live under a bridge like a troll or inside a cave like a goblin?

56

Would you rather live in the age of the dinosaurs or live in an age of magic?

57

Would you rather eat pizza with mushrooms as the only topping or eat cheeseburgers with only tomatoes on them?

58

Would you rather cut the grass with a pair of scissors or rake the leaves in your yard with a fork?

59

Would you rather drink a cup of snail slime or eat a live cricket?

60

Would you rather go on a treasure hunt for gold or hunt the biggest moose known to man?

61

Would you rather be a dog or a cat for a day?

62

Would you rather explore the jungle or the mountains?

63

Would you rather spend all day reading books or fishing in a pond?

64

Would you rather eat three pounds of spaghetti in one sitting or eat three pounds of strawberry cake over the course of a day?

65

Would you rather listen to the same song on repeat for an entire week or only listen to your favorite song once a month?

66

Would you rather always have a GPS handy for directions or always know where north is?

67

Would you rather jump on a trampoline nonstop for an entire day or only eat different kinds of soup for the rest of your life?

68

Would you rather have a boomerang that always comes back no matter how you throw it or a crown that makes its wearer tell the truth?

69

Would you rather trek through the Amazon rainforest or climb through the Himalayan mountains?

70

Would you rather live in a world where robots rule everything or live in a world where dogs could talk?

71

Would you rather only eat things made of chocolate for the rest of your life or have a side of orange peels with every meal?

72

Would you rather learn how to bake from the best baker in the world or learn how to play the violin from the world's best violinist?

73

Would you rather take your dogs on a walk through the Alaskan wilderness or take your dogs on a walk through the beaches of Panama?

74

Would you rather pick up every fallen leaf you see on a daily basis or water every plant you walk past?

75

Would you rather bathe in the slime of a slug or dance with a group of chimpanzees?

76

Would you rather shout "OUCH" every time you were hurt by someone (or something) or only speak to people when you are in pain?

77

Would you rather save a penny from every dollar you spend or spend a dollar for every penny you lose?

78

Would you rather have a candle that never loses its flame or have a bag of wind that could blow whenever you opened it?

79

Would you rather have a crystal ball that could predict the events of the next five minutes or have a magic lamp containing a genie who has the power to grant you three wishes?

80

Would you rather go swimming in the middle of the winter or go ice skating in the middle of the summer?

81

Would you rather learn how to throw an axe or learn how to sharpen a sword?

82

Would you rather have a pet gecko or a pet raccoon?

83

Would you rather have your own personal helicopter or your own personal jet?

84

Would you rather ride a horse on the beach or on the moon?

85

Would you rather have a conversation with an alien or have a conversation with a robot?

86

Would you rather hold a hot coal in the palm of your hands or get your tongue stuck to a street lamp pole?

87

Would you rather learn to solve a Rubik's cube or put together a jigsaw puzzle?

88

Would you rather eat a celery salad or drink a cucumber milkshake?

89

Would you rather have two right feet or have two right hands?

90

Would you rather grow your own food or make your own ice cream?

91

Would you rather have a bracelet made out of nickel or copper?

92

Would you rather go on a cruise across the seven seas or travel to see the seven wonders of the world?

93

Would you rather surf on the biggest wave recorded in history or ski down Mt. Everest?

94

Would you rather ride in a UFO or be the scientist who discovers a new element?

95

Would you rather have a coconut tree in your backyard or have a cactus in your backyard?

96

Would you rather live with a vampire or a werewolf?

97

Would you rather write the world's longest book or read the world's longest book?

98

Would you rather only have 8 fingers or have a total of 12 fingers?

99

Would you rather watch the sunset over the Grand Canyon or see the Northern Lights in Canada?

100

Would you rather walk to the store every time you needed to go there or ride your bike to and from school?

101

Would you rather drink hot chocolate at least once a day for the rest of your life or only have hot chocolate once every five years?

102

Would you rather eat a spoonful of black pepper or a spoonful of red pepper?

103

Would you rather run as fast as you can for an entire ten minutes or perform jumping jacks for an entire hour?

104

Would you rather live in a big city or live in the countryside?

105

Would you rather have the world's healthiest hair or the world's healthiest skin?

106

Would you rather go to school with your best friends or go to school with your cousins?

107

Would you rather pogo stick on the moon or jump on a trampoline beside a volcano?

108

Would you rather go dirt biking every weekend for a year or go swimming every day of the summer?

109

Would you rather have the fastest computer in the world or the fastest dog in the world?

110

Would you rather have very ugly clothes that never got dirty or great looking clothes you would have to dry clean every day?

111

Would you rather eat donuts or fruit for the rest of your life?

112

Would you rather have fingernails you never have to cut or hair you never have to wash?

113

Would you rather get your hand caught in the wheel of a bicycle or burn yourself while cooking?

114

Would you rather be scared in public while watching a scary movie or be scared in a haunted house all by yourself?

115

Would you rather dream the wildest dreams or remember the littlest things?

116

Would you rather have a gopher or a squirrel for a pet?

117

Would you rather be the main character in a blockbuster movie or the main character in an exciting book?

118

Would you rather stay young forever or have hair that never grows grey or white?

119

Would you rather take out the trash every day or do the dishes every day?

120

Would you rather make the tastiest waffles and never eat them or eat the tastiest waffles and never share them?

121

Would you rather play a game of chess or checkers with your favorite historical figure?

122

Would you rather have a telescope that can see invisible things or have a whistle that allowed you to speak to bees?

123

Would you rather have the world's fastest car but never drive it or drive the world's fastest car once and never own it?

124

Would you rather have a steak dinner with Harry Potter or have a milkshake with Tony Stark?

125

Would you rather never clean your room again or never play with your toys again?

Chapter 2

What Do You Have to Lose?

Can you think of a time where you lost something important (if you are anything like me, this has probably happened more than just once…)? What about how many times have you had to do without something? Or how many times have you *forgotten* something?

Well, this hilarious section of the book allows you to relive those exact moments!

The questions in this chapter will bring up some extremely funny situations. For example, you may find yourself having to give up something you love (or hate) for something different. You may also find yourself asking, *"Would I rather go without this or that?"* or even, *"Would I rather forget about this or that?"*

Heck, you may find yourself wondering if you can even answer a question at all.

With that being said, let's dive into these questions and explore some of the crazy choices that lie ahead of you!

Questions

1

Would you rather lose your sight or your hearing?

2

Would you rather only have the ability to speak or to read?

3

Would you rather have hair all over your body or have no hair at all?

4

Would you rather never drink milk ever again or only drink milk for the rest of your life?

5

Would you rather never wear shoes at all or wear shoes all the time for the rest of your life?

6

Would you rather forget your mom's name or never be able to say the word 'mom'?

7

Would you rather lose your ability to taste anything or lose your sense of smell?

8

Would you rather forget everything you ever learned in history class or remember everything you learned from English class?

9

Would you rather forget how to ride a bicycle or learn how to drink water through your nose?

10

Would you rather never be able to eat cheese again or only be able to eat corn for the rest of your life?

11

Would you rather never take a bath or never brush your teeth?

12

Would you rather lose your ability to sing or lose your ability to dance?

13

Would you rather go without food or go without water for a whole day?

14

Would you rather never worry about time again or always be on time?

15

Would you rather forget the name of your best friend or forget who your best friend is?

16

Would you rather never go on an airplane or never ride a train?

17

Would you rather never have milk with your cereal or always have cereal with your milk?

18

Would you rather never use a computer again or never use your phone again?

19

Would you rather lose all of your teeth or never eat cheeseburgers again?

20

Would you rather stop going to school or stop riding the bus?

21

Would you rather lose the ability to swim or lose the ability to ride a bike?

22

Would you rather forget where your notebook is or forget where your textbook is?

23

Would you rather lose a foot race or come in second at the science fair?

24

Would you rather never go to a baseball game or never go to a football game ever again?

25

Would you rather never drink soda or never drink orange juice for the rest of your life?

26

Would you rather forget where you left the TV remote or forget where you left your cell phone?

27

Would you rather forget how to microwave popcorn or forget how to bake pizza?

28

Would you rather lose all of your toys or your video games in a bet?

29

Would you rather forget everything you know about science or forget everything you know about math?

30

Would you rather forget how to play football or how to play kickball?

31

Would you rather forget your way home or forget your math homework?

32

Would you rather never eat turkey or never eat ham again?

33

Would you rather lose all your money and become the smartest person alive or lose all your intelligence and become the richest person alive?

34

Would you rather only be able to see out of your right eye or your left eye?

35

Would you rather give a piece of clothing away after you wear it for a day or always wear the same outfit every day?

36

Would you rather lose your ability to see the color red or lose your ability to taste spicy foods?

37

Would you rather forget everything you learned in second grade or forget everything you learned in kindergarten?

38

Would you rather forget what apple juice tastes like or forget how to eat boiled eggs?

39

Would you rather lose all of your teeth or lose all of your finger nails?

40

Would you rather stop going to the dentist or stop going to the doctor?

41

Would you rather not watch movies ever again or not play video games ever again?

42

Would you rather lose all sensation and feeling in your skin or in your teeth?

43

Would you rather forget what chocolate tastes like or forget what caramel tastes like?

44

Would you rather go without water when using the restroom for an entire day or go without eating for an entire day?

45

Would you rather never go fishing and hunting again or never play sports again?

46

Would you rather not have to do any homework for any of your classes or not have to go to school to pass your classes?

47

Would you rather give up on trying to learn something new or teach something new to a friend of yours?

48

Would you rather not have any pets or not have any friends?

49

Would you rather not have to practice for anything ever again or spend all of your time practicing what you love to do?

50

Would you rather lose all of your hair for an entire year or grow all of your fingernails for an entire year?

51

Would you rather give up all of your lunch money for a week or go a whole week without eating breakfast?

52

Would you rather never watch TV again or never listen to music again?

53

Would you rather swap out your sense of smell for tougher skin or swap out your sense of touch for a stronger sense of smell?

54

Would you rather never see a bug ever again or never see a rat ever again?

55

Would you rather have the ability to sing well or to act well?

56

Would you rather never eat another piece of broccoli or never eat cauliflower again?

57

Would you rather never own a parrot or never own an iguana as a pet?

58

Would you rather never experience another summer or never experience another winter again?

59

Would you rather forget where you left your shoes or forget where you left your belt?

60

Would you rather never see a clown again or never go to a rodeo again?

61

Would you rather never eat eggs or never drink milk again?

62

Would you rather never read comic books or never read science textbooks ever again?

63

Would you rather never go for a jog or never skateboard ever again?

64

Would you rather not have to go to class or not have to go to recess?

65

Would you rather not see anything or not hear certain sounds?

66

Would you rather never have to use soap or never have to use toothpaste again?

67

Would you rather never know if aliens exist or never know what lies at the bottom of the ocean?

68

Would you rather stop going to barbecues or stop going to roller rinks?

69

Would you rather quit eating hotdogs or quit eating pizza?

70

Would you rather not have fingers or not have toes?

71

Would you rather never have to do laundry again or never have to clean your room again?

72

Would you rather never eat another pickle or never eat another peach?

73

Would you rather not watch TV for a week or not listen to the radio for a week?

74

Would you rather not have homework assignments for a month or not ride in a car for a month?

75

Would you rather forget everything you know about dogs or forget everything you know about cats?

76

Would you rather never have to wear shorts or never have to wear shoes again?

77

Would you rather never own a car or never own a house?

78

Would you rather never fly in an airplane or never ride in a boat?

79

Would you rather never sleep again or never have to eat breakfast again?

80

Would you rather not obey the laws of gravity or not be able to move at all?

81

Would you rather never have learned to read or never have learned to write?

82

Would you rather not go to the store again or never see another star again?

83

Would you rather forget how to make a sandwich or forget how to make your bed?

84

Would you rather never eat fast food again or never drink grape juice again?

85

Would you rather not be able to play sports again or not be able to learn new things?

86

Would you rather never eat cheese or never eat tomato soup again?

87

Would you rather never play musical chairs or never play backgammon again?

88

Would you rather rather never look at a tree or never look at a flower again?

89

Would you rather never floss your teeth or never apply sunscreen ever again?

90

Would you rather not know how someone feels or not know the definition of a word you use in a sentence?

91

Would you rather never take another test ever again or choose the tests assigned in class?

92

Would you rather never eat candy or never drink soda again?

93

Would you rather never watch cartoons or never watch sports again?

94

Would you rather stop going to the doctor's office or stop taking medicine?

95

Would you rather stop listening to what people have to say or have people stop listening to what you have to say?

96

Would you rather never eat Doritos or never eat Cheetos for the rest of your life?

97

Would you rather never wear pajamas again or wear pajamas every day for the rest of your life?

98

Would you rather not have to plug your computer into an outlet or not have to write anything ever again?

99

Would you rather lose all your teeth or lose all your arm hair?

100

Would you rather never fly a paper airplane again or lose the ability to tear paper?

101

Would you rather forget all of your memories about fish or forget how to catch a fish?

102

Would you rather give up your most prized possession or give someone their most prized possession?

103

Would you rather forget what a zebra looks like or forget what a crocodile looks like?

104

Would you rather have to give away a copy of your favorite book to a friend or give it to a stranger?

105

Would you rather be able to tell the difference between a wolf and a dog or a lynx and a cat?

106

Would you rather not remember the color of a starfish or how to use a sponge?

107

Would you rather forget how to read a clock or forget how to count to 100?

108

Would you rather never fly a kite again or never go bowling again?

109

Would you rather forget what you know about bigfoot or forget what you know about the Loch Ness monster?

110

Would you rather forget how to drink from a glass or forget how to eat with a fork?

111

Would you rather not remember what ham smells like or not remember what a pumpkin smells like?

112

Would you rather never be able to look in the mirror again or never be able to open a door again?

113

Would you rather not be able to tell when someone is upset with you or not be able to make up with someone who is upset or angry with you?

114

Would you rather forget the last thing you watched on TV or forget the last thing you learned in a classroom?

115

Would you rather lose your eyebrows or lose the ability to smile?

116

Would you rather forget how to light a candle or forget how to cook ramen noodles?

117

Would you rather lose track of time for an entire week or lose your favorite watch forever?

118

Would you rather not play video games for a whole week or not eat tacos for a whole week?

119

Would you rather not be able to sing your favorite songs or not be able to tell your favorite stories?

120

Would you rather forget the name of your favorite teacher or forget the name of your school?

121

Would you rather forget the password to your computer or forget how to spell your last name?

122

Would you rather not smell anything for the rest of your life or take the trash out for the rest of your life?

123

Would you rather forget how to read a map or forget how to do long division?

124

Would you rather lose track of all of your favorite things or help people find the things they lose?

125

Would you rather only eat vegetables or only be allowed to eat chocolate?

Chapter 3

What Could You Do?

What *could* you do?

Have you ever wondered what type of superpower you would like to have? Are there more than one?

Is there anything about your favorite animal that you think is really cool? Cool enough to have on your own body?

Or what if you had access to something so amazing that it made you the most special person on earth?

Well, in this section, you will be figuring these exact things out because these questions will put your *abilities* to the test.

Now, there is something important to mention about the questions in this chapter – make sure you don't hold back. You may find that there are questions that will have you altering your body. In this manner, you may become a stronger (and yes, a sillier) version of yourself.

Remember, with great power comes great responsibility.

So, let's dive into the questions and see what kinds of powers await.

Questions

1

Would you rather be able to fly or turn invisible?

2

Would you rather have the sight of an eagle or the teeth of a shark?

3

Would you rather have wings like a bird or horns like a ram?

4

Would you rather have x-ray vision or supersonic hearing?

5

Would you rather only be able to walk backwards or only be able to speak in Latin?

6

Would you rather be able to read minds or predict the future?

7

Would you rather control electricity or have the power to control shadows?

8

Would you rather be able to spray lemonade out of your fingertips or identify any plant by smell?

9

Would you rather be able to float for as long as you want or jump as high as you want?

10

Would you rather be able to write with your index finger as if it were a pen or talk to people telepathically?

11

Would you rather have the hearing of a bat or a wolf's sense of smell?

12

Would you rather be a hundred feet tall or the size of an ant?

13

Would you rather be able to remember every single dream you have ever had or remember every single person you have ever met?

14

Would you rather be able to tell whenever anyone is lying or make everyone believe in anything you say?

15

Would you rather live on land, as well as in water, or be able to survive only in water?

16

Would you rather have control over fire or control over ice?

17

Would you rather know what is in a book by just looking at the cover or be able to type with your mind?

18

Would you rather have mac and cheese whenever you want or be able to cook the perfect grilled cheese sandwich?

19

Would you rather be the fastest runner in the world or be the highest jumper in the world?

20

Would you rather have the strength of a bear or the speed of a cheetah?

21

Would you rather have skin as hard as cement or weigh as light as a feather?

22

Would you rather be able to track any animal or find any criminal?

23

Would you rather never have to eat food or get any delicious food you can imagine instantly?

24

Would you rather be able to magnetize any metal or make metal appear out of thin air?

25

Would you rather have the ability to teleport wherever you want or be able to stop time?

26

Would you rather leap across any distance or fit into any space?

27

Would you rather be able to draw anything from memory or sculpt the world's best sculptures?

28

Would you rather be able to fit anything into your pockets or remember the most bizarre facts?

29

Would you rather possess the world's stretchiest skin or be able to eat anything for nourishment?

30

Would you rather be the fastest talker alive or have the ability to cook a good meal with any ingredient?

31

Would you rather be able to turn your sense of smell on and off at will or determine the origin of every smell?

32

Would you rather know where every bug is at all times or be able to talk to bugs?

33

Would you rather have the ability to fix anything that is broken or tear anything you want in half?

34

Would you rather change your hair color like a chameleon or slither like a snake?

35

Would you rather go to sleep for months at a time and feel rested for the rest of the year or have never ending energy?

36

Would you rather be able to make smoke appear from your hands or dissolve into smoke and disappear?

37

Would you rather have the ability to zoom into things you see or have the world's most high-tech camera?

38

Would you rather be able to breathe underwater or jump as high as a skyscraper?

39

Would you rather intimidate anyone just by winking at them or never be intimidated yourself?

40

Would you rather be able to smell the color orange or the color green?

41

Would you rather have skin that never gets cold or skin that never grows old?

42

Would you rather have feathers like a pigeon or fur like a fox?

43

Would you rather identify any language just by hearing it or speak any language you wish?

44

Would you rather always explain your point or always understand what people are trying to say?

45

Would you rather have the ability to never become tired or have the ability to always get a good night's sleep?

46

Would you rather have indestructible teeth or eyes that never get dry?

47

Would you rather have the skin of a rhinoceros or the antlers of a moose?

48

Would you rather control fish with your mind or have rats obey your every command?

49

Would you rather be able to tell the temperature just by exposing your skin or always know where the moon is in the sky?

50

Would you rather have the ability to charge electronic objects just by touching them or always know what's playing on TV?

51

Would you rather know the definition of every word in the English language or write the most beautiful songs?

52

Would you rather be able to make any liquid cold at any time or make ice appear out of thin air?

53

Would you rather grow strawberries from the tips of your fingers or grow blueberries from the tips of your toes?

54

Would you rather be able to spit lemon juice or hot sauce whenever you wanted?

55

Would you rather grow mushrooms wherever you want or know where every single ant hill in the world is located?

56

Would you rather be as fast as lightning or as quick as quicksand?

57

Would you rather know the answer to any math question or have the ability to identify whose handwriting it is just by looking at it?

58

Would you rather never lose your breath or never be thirsty?

59

Would you rather style your hair however you want with nothing at all or change the color of your skin at will?

60

Would you rather be able to tell when someone is lying or be able to learn anything you want in an hour?

61

Would you rather be able to count money just by looking at it or be able to tell if fruit is ripe just by looking at it?

62

Would you rather be the fastest reader in the world or the fastest writer in the world?

63

Would you rather paint brilliant masterpieces in one sitting or sing like the best singers in the world?

64

Would you rather get your nutrients through photosynthesis like a flower or radiate light like the sun?

65

Would you rather control bees by making clicking noises with your tongue or tell grasshoppers where to go just by pointing in a direction?

66

Would you rather talk to people without moving your mouth or know what someone wants just by looking at their face?

67

Would you rather be able to fly only during night time or only during daytime?

68

Would you rather prevent people from fighting just by looking at them or upset others just by smiling at them?

69

Would you rather be able to see other people's memories or grant one person any wish?

70

Would you rather make flowers bloom just by touching them or make someone into a tree by pointing at them?

71

Would you rather skydive without a parachute or bungee jump without a bungee cord?

72

Would you rather create slime like a slug just by sweating or be able to hunt like a wolf?

73

Would you rather be able to program any computer or solve a problem using any cell phone?

74

Would you rather have a shirt that can change to any color you wish or have a pair of pants that can change into any fabric you like?

75

Would you rather have a glass bottle that can change water into any drink you want or have a lunch box that can serve your favourite foods the moment you have a craving?

76

Would you rather have skin as hard as a brick or fingers as flexible as elastic bands?

77

Would you rather be able to see no matter how dark it is or be able to whisper to people from across the room?

78

Would you rather be able to make fresh muffins appear out of thin air or be able to turn any glass of water into tea?

79

Would you rather have a parrot who can repeat anything it hears or a lizard that sticks to any surface?

80

Would you rather be able to drink any liquid as hydration or replicate any sculpture perfectly?

81

Would you rather have a pair of gloves that allows you to lift any object or a belt that allows you to hold any object?

82

Would you rather have a cup that is never empty or build a bar that serves any beverage you want?

83

Would you rather be able to fly or turn invisible?

84

Would you rather have a pair of shoes that allow you to bounce as if you were on springs or be able to walk across water?

85

Would you rather have feet as big as an ape or teeth as sharp as a piranha?

86

Would you rather have the ability to control machines or have the ability to shoot fireworks out of your nose?

87

Would you rather know where every precious gem in the world is or have one stone that can turn into any gem?

88

Would you rather have a matchbox that never runs out of matches or have a swiss army knife that never gets dull?

89

Would you rather have the ability to stretch your legs as long as you want or have the ability to not feel temperature in your hands?

90

Would you rather set the record for having the world's longest frisbee throw or the world's longest long jump?

91

Would you rather have a paintbrush that can paint in any color or have a canvas that makes paintings come to life?

92

Would you rather sing opera or only sing one song ever?

93

Would you rather have the car of your dreams or run faster than a car?

94

Would you rather have the wings of a bat or the tongue of a frog?

95

Would you rather have a clone of yourself or know what anyone around you is thinking?

96

Would you rather have a lantern that always stays lit or have a compass that always leads you to the snack you want?

97

Would you rather be small enough to live in a flower garden or live in a big tree house?

98

Would you rather be friends with the world's strongest person or the world's smartest person?

99

Would you rather have skin that doesn't get affected by fire or extinguish any flame just by blowing on it?

100

Would you rather have infinite wealth or be the most beautiful person on earth?

101

Would you rather know how to play the flute like an expert or have a flute that plays on its own?

102

Would you rather be able to jump inside paintings or be able to take pictures with your eyes?

103

Would you rather be the loudest person in the room or be able to make anyone zip their lips?

104

Would you rather be friends with the fastest horse in the world or be friends with the fattest cat ever?

105

Would you rather have a clock that never makes you late or have an oven that always has a fresh batch of cookies ready?

106

Would you rather have a brain freeze or never eat your favorite ice cream again?

107

Would you rather be a mouse free in a field or a mouse living in a castle?

108

Would you rather be able to remember the names of each of the 50 states in America or be able to name each country in the world?

109

Would you rather be the best superhero in the world or the best friend in the world?

110

Would you rather have the ability to find any lost object or to hide any object without anyone finding it?

111

Would you rather know the deepest secret the world has to offer or not be able to tell the truth?

112

Would you rather be a worm that lives in an apple or accidentally eat a worm in an apple?

113

Would you rather run as fast as a jaguar or own a Jaguar sports car?

114

Would you rather be the ceiling or the floor?

115

Would you rather be an ugly sweater or a pair of inflatable pants?

116

Would you rather grow bark on top of your skin like a tree or have leaves that sprout from your head instead of hair?

117

Would you rather have the ears of a dog or the tongue of a cat?

118

Would you rather be able to grow your hair as fast as you want or have hair that can never be destroyed?

119

Would you rather be able to hear what animals are thinking or smell what animals are smelling?

120

Would you rather be a plant or never have to eat vegetables again?

121

Would you rather have a book that gives you the answer to any question or have a notebook that makes the things you wrote in it real?

122

Would you rather meet your favorite band or only listen to one of their songs forever?

123

Would you rather grow scales like a snake or have eyes like an owl?

124

Would you rather be able to always hit your target with a bow and arrow or never shop at Target again?

125

Would you rather have a key that unlocks any door or have a mirror that can show hidden objects?

Chapter 4

What If?

Have you ever found yourself asking someone, *"What do you think would happen if...?"*

If you are anything like me, then I am sure you have.

These types of questions are great because they feed both your curiosity and your imagination. They make you imagine what it would feel like if you were someone (or even *something*) completely different.

They can help you see yourself living a life that is not your own, or as someone or something different from what you see in the mirror.

And let's admit it – it's fun to do that.

In this chapter, you may find yourself facing some truly bizarre questions. But don't be afraid to answer them – these questions will have you reimagining yourself in ways you never thought possible.

So, prepare for some laughs, and let's see what kinds of fantasies await!

Questions

1

If you could only eat one thing for the rest of your life, would you rather only eat Neapolitan ice cream or clam chowder?

2

If you were a mermaid who lived in the sea, would you rather have the head of a fish or the tail of a fish?

3

If you were a robot, would you rather have robot legs that walk or wheels to move around?

4

If you had wings, would you rather have the wings of a bird or the wings of an airplane?

5

If you had the smartest mind in the world, would you rather be a mathematician or a historian?

6

If you were a vehicle, would you rather be a car, a train, or an airplane?

7

If you were a string instrument, would you rather be a guitar or a banjo?

8

If you were a planet, would you rather be made completely of gas or have rings around you?

9

If you were a dragon, would you rather breathe fire or ice?

10

If you had to choose one sandwich to eat for the rest of your life, would you rather eat peanut butter and jelly or ham and cheese?

11

If you were a bird, would you rather be a bluebird or a cardinal?

12

If you were an artist, would you rather be a painter or a sculptor?

13

If you were an astronaut, would you rather go to the moon or go to Mars?

14

If you were a fruit, would you rather have seeds or be seedless?

15

If you were a toy, would you rather be made out of plastic or cotton?

16

If you had an unusual pet, would you rather have a dinosaur or an ostrich?

17

If you owned a car, would you rather own a sports car or a monster truck?

18

If you were a famous athlete, would you rather be a professional golfer or a professional basketball player?

19

If you were in a cartoon, would you rather be an animal or a robot?

20

If you had needles sticking out of you, would you rather be a cactus or a porcupine?

21

If you were a dog, would you rather be a golden retriever or a beagle?

22

If you were a tree, would you rather be in the forest or in someone's yard?

23

If you were a rock, would you rather be thrown into a lake or thrown into a canyon?

24

If you were a light bulb, would you rather be a white light or a yellow light?

25

If you were one of Santa's elves, would you rather wear red or wear green?

26

If you lived in a swamp, would you rather live in a boat or live in a shack?

27

If you forgot your name, would you rather have your parents give you another one or come up with the name yourself?

28

If you were a wizard, would you rather use your powers to defy gravity or control anyone you wanted?

29

If the weather changed according to your emotions, would you rather it be rainy when you are sad or sunny when you are sad?

30

If you lived on a beach, would you rather surf all day or hunt sharks all day?

31

If you could travel through time, would you rather go back to the age of dinosaurs or go back to the industrial revolution?

32

If you were a car, would you rather be an electric car or a gas car?

33

If you were an ant, would you rather be a black ant or a red ant?

34

If you were a cowboy, would you rather ride horseback or ride on a train?

35

If you lived in ancient Japan, would you rather be a samurai or a ninja?

36

If you were a cookie, would you rather be a chocolate chip cookie or a sugar cookie?

37

If you were a reptile, would you rather be a lizard or a frog?

38

If you were an alien, would you rather have green skin or gray skin?

39

If you were a flower, would you rather be a rose or a violet?

40

If you lived in a garden, would you rather be a butterfly or a caterpillar?

41

If you were a tree, would you rather grow plums or peaches?

42

If you were a statue, would you rather be made of stone or metal?

43

If you could choose, would you rather be the world's tallest person or the world's shortest person?

44

If your skin were an abnormal color, would you rather have red skin or blue skin?

45

If you were a dinosaur, would you rather be a brontosaurus or a pterodactyl?

46

If you were a feline, would you rather be a mountain lion or a jaguar?

47

If you were one of the smartest scientists in the world, would you rather work on chemistry or physics?

48

If you were a captain, would you rather be the captain of a boat or the captain of an airplane?

49

If you were a kung fu artist, would you rather know jiu jitsu or taekwondo?

50

If you were an inventor, would you rather have invented electricity or the internet?

51

If you could choose one sport to play for the rest of your life, would you rather play badminton or hockey?

52

If you could choose one city to vacation in, would you rather choose London or Paris?

53

If you could choose one place to live for the rest of your life, would you rather live in the swamps or the mountains?

54

If you were a monkey, would you rather be a gorilla or an orangutan?

55

If you were an outlaw, would you rather be a bank robber or a train robber?

56

If you were the world's best liar, would you rather convince people you were smart or convince people you were rich?

57

If you were an actor in a play, would you rather be on Broadway or at your local theater?

58

If you could only eat one breakfast item for the rest of your life, would you rather eat a breakfast burrito or a breakfast muffin sandwich?

59

If you could teleport yourself wherever you wanted, would you rather teleport yourself to an art museum or to a park?

60

If you could live in a movie, would you rather live in Jurassic Park or in the Avengers?

61

If you were to win an award, would you rather win it for "Best Dressed" or "Most Likely to Succeed?"

62

If you had to choose, would you rather have a black eye or a swollen lip?

63

If you lived on Mars, would you rather get around in a dune buggy or on a hoverboard?

64

If you could travel through time, would you rather travel to the past or to the future?

65

If you were a master chef and could choose any cuisine to master, would you rather cook Japanese food or Italian food?

66

If you had to play one board game for the rest of your life, would you rather play Monopoly or Clue?

67

If you could choose the color of your natural hair, would you rather be a brunette, a red head, or a blonde?

68

If you had superpowers, would you rather be a superhero or a super villain?

69

If you were a mythical creature, would you rather be a centaur or a minotaur?

70

If you could fly, would you rather have wings or be able to float?

71

If you could choose one pie to eat for the rest of your life, would you rather eat cherry or apple?

72

If you were to have a sea creature as a pet, would you rather want a narwhal or an octopus?

73

If you could only drink one soda for the rest of your life, would you rather drink root beer or red cream soda?

74

If you could only watch one cartoon for the rest of your life, would you rather watch Scooby Doo or the Jetsons?

75

If you could speak to one type of insect, would you rather speak with crickets or ants?

76

If you had to choose to only do one for the rest of your life, would you rather choose skateboarding or rollerblading?

77

If you had to choose a food to eat for an entire month, would you rather eat hamburgers or hotdogs?

78

If you were a unicorn, would you rather have a rainbow mane or be able to ride rainbows?

79

If you were a radio host, would you rather play rock and roll music or jazz music?

80

If you were a sports announcer, would you rather be a really loud one or a really quiet one?

81

If you found the gold at the end of a leprechauns rainbow, would you rather keep all the money for yourself or share some with your family and friends?

82

If you lived in medieval times and were a knight, would you rather fight with a bow or a sword?

83

If you were an expert on animals, would you rather know everything about anteaters or groundhogs?

84

If you were a geologist, would you rather study the volcanoes on Hawaii or in the Grand Canyon?

85

If you were an artist, would you rather paint pictures of people or paint pictures of different landscapes?

86

If you were a cyclops, would you rather have super strength or super vision?

87

If you lived on an island, would you rather it be inhabited by coconut trees or mango trees?

88

If you were an airplane pilot, would you rather pilot a private jet or a spy plane?

89

If you could relive one year of your life, would you rather relive when you were five or relive when you were ten?

90

If you could read minds, would you rather read your mother's mind or your father's mind?

91

If you could spend one million dollars on one thing, would you rather buy a jet pack or a robotic dog?

92

If you owned a farm, would you rather grow turnips or radishes?

93

If you worked in a restaurant, would you rather be the chef or wash the dishes?

94

If you lived on the beach, would you rather be a crab or a starfish?

95

If you were a mountain, would you rather be in the Appalachians or in the Rockies?

96

If you could travel to one country for free, would you rather go to Ireland or Ukraine?

97

If you were a house, would you rather be made
of wood or be made of brick?

98

If you were a comedian, would you rather act in
a movie or tell jokes on a big stage?

99

If you were five years older, would you rather
be living in the same house you are now or be
living in a house you used to live in?

100

If you were a bat, would you rather be a
vampire bat or a fruit bat?

101

If you were a chef, would you rather serve the Queen of England her favorite dish or a brand new dish?

102

If you were a baseball player, would you rather swing with a wooden baseball bat or an aluminum baseball bat?

103

If you were a flower, would you rather have different colored petals or similar colored petals?

104

If you were a t-shirt, would you rather be short-sleeved or long-sleeved?

105

If you were a person who owned a dog farm, would you rather name each one of your dogs personally or have people send you letters with name ideas for the dogs?

106

If you were a pizza, would you rather be cheese or pepperoni?

107

If you were a spider, would you rather be a banana spider or a tarantula?

108

If you were a toothbrush, would you rather clean teeth or toilets?

109

If you were a baker, would you rather bake cheesecakes for the rest of your life or bake key lime pies for the rest of your life?

110

If you were a hero, would you rather have an unbreakable sword or an unbreakable shield?

111

If you were the fastest person in the world, would you rather be an Olympic runner or a pizza delivery person?

112

If you were water, would you rather be ice, liquid, or gas?

113

If you had two heads, would you rather they both think from the same brain or each think from different brains?

114

If you were a dog, would you rather have a pink nose or a black nose?

115

If you were a magician, would you rather saw your assistant in half or pull a bunny out of a hat?

116

If you were a mutant, would you rather have ten arms or ten legs?

117

If you were a famous musician, would you rather perform your songs at large concerts or small coffee shops?

118

If you could choose the color of your eyes, would you rather have brown eyes or green eyes?

119

If you were only allowed to wear one pair of pants for the rest of your life, would you rather wear sweatpants or jeans?

120

If you were a clown, would you rather work in a rodeo or a circus?

121

If you were a dentist, would you rather floss or clean the teeth of your patients?

122

If you were pig, would you rather lay in the mud all day or sleep on a bale of hay?

123

If you were a bus driver, would you rather drive a school bus or a public transit bus?

124

If you worked at an amusement park, would you rather work the roller coasters or the water slides?

125

If you had four arms, would you rather cut two extra holes in every one of your shirts or never wear shirts again?

Conclusion

Absolutely amazing work – you have made it all the way to the conclusion.

Now that you are here, we have a couple of final questions to finish with:

- Did you answer each of the 500 questions contained in this book truthfully?

- Did you do your best to make sure the family and friends you asked answered truthfully, too?

- Did you have fun?

- Did you learn something new about yourself?

- Did you learn something new about your family and friends?

If you can answer yes to each of these questions, then congratulations – you have done a fantastic job!

But you may be wondering, does that mean the party is over?

And I am happy to say, NO, of course not!

You see, what is stopping you from asking these same questions to different people who have never read this book before?

Nothing!

So, don't just set the book down and never open it up again. Make sure you put its questions to use.

Memorize a few of your favorite questions and ask them to your grandma the next time you see her. Ask your cousin, your teacher, or even the people you meet at the grocery store.

Remember, questions will always lead to answers, so don't ever be afraid to ask questions.

And of course, questions don't have to come from this book. Now that you have made it to the end, you should have a taste of what makes a good question – so go ahead and make up some of your own.

And do me a favor – try and make them even sillier than the ones on this book!

Made in the USA
Middletown, DE
09 April 2020